REASONING SKILLS IN MATHS

Years 1 & 2

Talk it, solve it

by Jennie Pennant

with Rachel Bradley and Jacky Walters

We would like to thank the following schools in Bracknell Forest for trialling these activities:

Ascot Heath Infant	Meadow Vale Primary
Ascot Heath CE Junior	New Scotland Hill Primary
Binfield CE Primary	Owlsmoor Primary
Birch Hill Primary	The Pines Primary
Broadmoor Primary	Sandy Lane Primary and Nursery
College Town Infant	St Joseph's Catholic Primary
College Town Junior	St Margaret Clitherow Catholic Primary
Cranbourne Primary	St Michael's CE Primary
Crown Wood Primary	St Michael's Easthampstead CE VA Primary
Crowthorne CE Primary	Uplands Primary
Fox Hill Primary	Warfield CE Primary
Great Hollands Primary	Whitegrove Primary
Harmans Water Primary	Wildridings Primary
Holly Spring Infant and Nursery	Winkfield St Mary's CE Primary
Holly Spring Junior	Wooden Hill Primary and Nursery

We would also like to thank the BEAM Development Group.

BEAM Education

BEAM Education is a specialist mathematics education publisher, dedicated to promoting the teaching and learning of mathematics as interesting, challenging and enjoyable. Their materials cover teaching and learning needs from the age of 3 to 14 and they offer consultancy and training.

BEAM is an acknowledged expert in the field of mathematics education.

BEAM Education
Maze Workshops
72a Southgate Road
London N1 3JT
Telephone 020 7684 3323
Fax 020 7684 3334
Email info@beam.co.uk
www.beam.co.uk

Published by BEAM Education

Reprinted 2008.

ISBN 978 1 9031 4276 9
British Library Cataloguing-in-Publication Data
Data available
Edited by Raewyn Glynn
Designed by Malena Wilson-Max
Printed in Hong Kong by Paramount Printing Co. Ltd

Contents

Preface

Our primary teachers in Bracknell Forest have developed these collaborative activities to give children aged 5–11 more opportunities to engage in meaningful mathematical discussion. They have ensured that talking and working together are central to the activities, and have trialled them extensively in our primary schools to make sure that they work. Teachers reported that the children engaged enthusiastically in the dialogue, and in the thinking that ensued.

The main objective is to get children talking about mathematics. The context for this is logical thinking and reasoning, because there is scope here for debating more closely mathematical definitions, properties and patterns. Our teachers observed that the children did question each other, and wanted justifications, before they reached consensus.

We, in Bracknell Forest, hope that these activities will support and stimulate colleagues in promoting mathematical talk in the classroom, and that children's enjoyment and understanding of mathematics will be enhanced as a result. Many thanks to the teachers, and children, who took part in the development of these materials.

A. Fletcher

Allison Fletcher

Assistant Director
Education, Children's Services and Libraries
Bracknell Forest

Introduction

Recent initiatives in mathematics teaching emphasise the importance of mathematical discussion within problem-solving, and within mathematical learning generally. Children learn maths by doing it and talking about it, hence language is integral to securing mathematical learning. The activities in this book require children to focus on speaking and listening, and on reasoning, as they interpret clues and identify which items to eliminate.

When we talk, we engage in dialogue with others, and we receive feedback from them. We want children to be involved in mathematical dialogue to help them explore, investigate, challenge, evaluate and actively construct mathematical meaning. When children work together in a small group, they can articulate their thinking, listen to one another and support each other's learning in a safe situation. Organising problem-solving in small groups increases the potential for developing the skills of speaking, listening and working together.

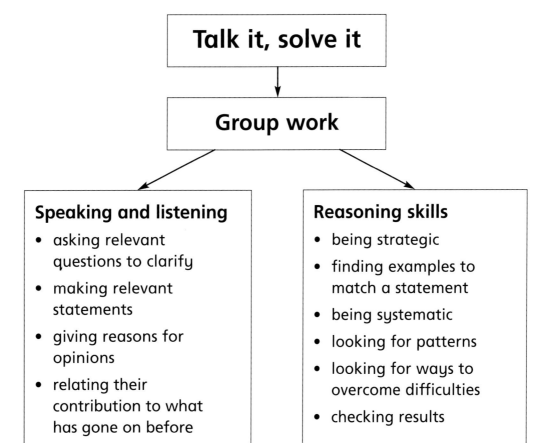

Talk it, solve it

↓

Group work

Speaking and listening
- asking relevant questions to clarify
- making relevant statements
- giving reasons for opinions
- relating their contribution to what has gone on before

Reasoning skills
- being strategic
- finding examples to match a statement
- being systematic
- looking for patterns
- looking for ways to overcome difficulties
- checking results

The 'Talk it, solve it' activities

In these activities, children identify an unknown item (number, shape, amount and so on) by means of clues, or questions and answers.

Each unit contains:

- a 'Solve it' sheet giving a collection of six items, one of which is the unknown item.

- a 'Talk it' sheet with six clues. These clues give enough information (and more) to identify this unknown item.

- an 'Ask it' sheet with a set of questions. Children choose their own item for others to identify, and the rest of the group ask the questions to discover the unknown item. Some of the questions are deliberately left open by including a blank space where children can insert their own number, shape, amount or other item.

The first unit consists of the 'Solve it' sheet, three different 'Talk it' clue sheets, and an 'Ask it' sheet. This unit will enable you to introduce the activity to the whole class, and to give the class confidence in using clues logically and effectively.

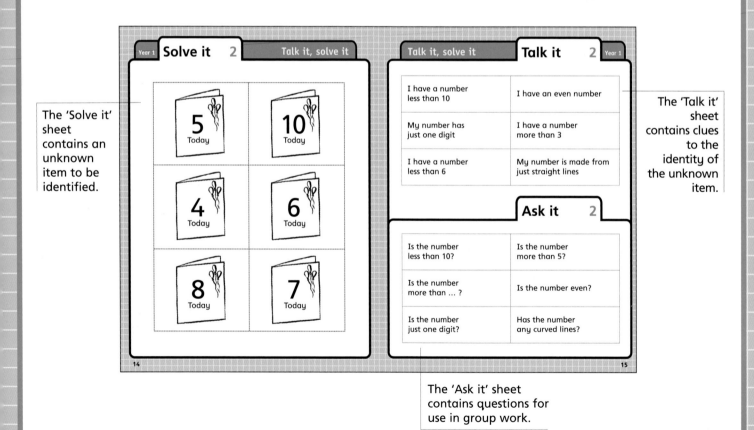

The 'Solve it' sheet contains an unknown item to be identified.

The 'Talk it' sheet contains clues to the identity of the unknown item.

The 'Ask it' sheet contains questions for use in group work.

Introducing the activity to the whole class

The 'Talk it' and 'Solve it' sheets

Display the 'Solve it' sheet on the whiteboard or overhead projector. Alternatively, if these are not available, give each pair of children a copy of the 'Solve it' sheet. Look at the numbers (or other items) shown and invite the children to identify some of the properties of the items. Support their observations by asking questions such as "Do you think that number is an even number? I wonder if you can see any other even numbers?"

Display the 'Talk it' sheet, look at the clues shown and talk about them briefly, or read out each statement in turn. You may choose to use the opportunity to check that children understand the mathematical content of the clues. Discuss with the class how to use these statements to eliminate items on the 'Solve it' sheet.

Choose one statement from the 'Talk it' sheet and cross out any eliminated items on the 'Solve it' sheet as they are identified. Continue like this until there is one item left. Go through any remaining clues as a check. If any statements don't fit, challenge the class to redress this or rethink.

The answers to the 'Solve it' sheets can be found on page 36 (for Year 1) and on page 64 (for Year 2).

The 'Ask it' sheet

Display the 'Ask it' sheet and read through the questions. Tell the children you are going to think of an item on the 'Solve it' sheet. They must ask you questions to discover the item you have secretly chosen. Discuss with the children which items to eliminate from the 'Solve it' sheet for each question.

When they have worked out your item, invite a pair of children to choose a secret item from the 'Solve it' sheet. Other pairs decide which questions to ask to find out the secret item. Talk with the children about the best questions to ask.

Working in pairs or small groups

Each group will need the 'Solve it' sheet to share between them, and the 'Talk it' sheet cut into strips. Ask the children to take it in turns to choose a 'Talk it' strip, read it to the group and together decide which item to eliminate on the 'Solve it' sheet. The children should keep taking turns until they have only one item left on the 'Solve it' sheet. Extend the activity by asking the group to establish if all the 'Talk it' statements are equally important. Ask if some statements eliminate more possibilities than others. Ask how few statements they can use to solve the problem. These questions could be used as a basis for a plenary discussion.

Meeting diverse needs

Children who need additional support

The activity can be adapted for children who need additional support by asking them to take a 'Talk it' strip and match it to one of the items on the 'Solve it' sheet. The activity then becomes one of identifying properties of a number, shape or other item.

For those who can manage a further challenge, put the cut 'Talk it' strips in a pile and invite children to pick the top one from the pile. Talk this through to decide which items it could refer to. Dealing with one clue at a time is simpler for inexperienced children than choosing a strip from the complete range.

More able learners

Suggest that children explore which of the 'Talk it' statements is the most informative and eliminates most items. When they have identified the unknown item on the 'Solve it' sheet, they should try again and find how many different routes there are through to that solution, including the shortest and the longest.

Invite them to invent their own questions as well as using those on the 'Ask it' sheet. Pairs can invent their own 'Solve it' sheet and a set of clues for other pairs to solve.

Those learning English as an additional language

Adapt the activity by helping children to organise themselves. Provide two sheets of paper labelled 'maybe' and 'no'. Cut the 'Solve it' sheet into six pieces and put them all on the 'maybe' paper. Then, as the 'Talk it' clues are read out, children can move the 'Solve it' items on to the 'no' paper.

Setting up the activity in this way provides a lot of helpful repetitious questions and statements.

Using the CD-ROM

The CD-ROM contains all the activity sets in the book. You can either project individual pages onto a whiteboard from your computer or print them out onto acetate sheets and use them on an overhead projector. You can also print the sheets out from the CD rather than making photocopies.

Year 1

Unit 1
Properties of 2D shapes

Unit 1 consists of the 'Solve it' sheet, three different 'Talk it' clue sheets and an 'Ask it' sheet. This unit will enable you to introduce the activity to the whole class, and to give the class confidence in using clues logically and effectively.

Talk it 1a

I have three feet	I have curly antennae
I have a rectangle for a nose	I have a straight mouth
I have round eyes	I have triangles for feet

Talk it 1b

I have a pointed nose	I have a curved mouth
My antennae are curled	I have circles for feet
My eyes are circles	I have got fewer than four feet

I have a straight mouth	I have a nose with four corners
I have curly antennae	I have square eyes
I have not got a curved mouth	I have three feet

Ask it 1

Has it got three feet?	Has it got a rectangle for a nose?
Has it got a straight mouth?	Has it got ... feet?
Has it got ... antennae?	Has it got ... eyes?

Talk it 2

I have a number less than 10	I have an even number
My number has just one digit	I have a number more than 3
I have a number less than 6	My number is made from just straight lines

Ask it 2

Is the number less than 10?	Is the number more than 5?
Is the number more than … ?	Is the number even?
Is the number just one digit?	Has the number any curved lines?

Talk it   3

I am more than 5 years old	My age is an even number
When you count in twos you say my age	My badge has two digits
I am younger than 15	I am not 10 years old

Ask it   3

Are they more than 5 years old?	Are they less than … years old?
Are they more than … years old?	Is their age an even number?
When you count in twos do you say their age?	Has their badge just one digit?

Talk it   4

I am not bus number 20	My number has just one digit
Add 2 to my number and the answer is less than 10	My number is between 4 and 9
Double my number and the answer is more than 10	My number is odd

Ask it   4

Is the bus number more than 10?	Is it bus number … ?
Has its number just one digit?	Is the number between 4 and … ?
If I add 2 to the number is the answer less than 10?	Is the number odd?

Talk it 5

My number is between 9 and 15	If you count in twos from 1 you will say my number
My number is odd	My number is less than 20
My number is more than 11	My number has two digits

Ask it 5

Has the number got two digits?	Is the number odd?
If I count in twos from 1 will I say the number?	Is the number between … and … ?
Is the number more than … ?	Is the number less than … ?

Talk it 6 Year 1

My nose is a circle	My nose is not a triangle
My eyes are not circles	My nose is not black
My buttons are square	My nose is round

Ask it 6

Is its nose a circle?	Is its nose … ?
Are its eyes triangles?	Are its eyes … ?
Are its buttons square?	Are its buttons … ?

Talk it 7

I have a circle on the end of my tail	My body is curved
My head is shaped like a triangle	My body is not a rectangle
My tail is straight	I have four legs

Ask it 7

Is there a circle on the end of the tail?	Is the body curved?
Is the body a rectangle?	Is the head shaped like a … ?
Is the tail straight?	Are the legs rectangles?

The ball is beside the box

The cat is outside the box

The car is in front of the box

The mouse is next to the ball

The cat is called Pushkin

The car is near the box

Ask it 8

Is the ball beside the box?

Is the ball ... the box?

Is the mouse next to the ... ?

Is the cat ... the box?

Is the car ... the box?

Is the car ... ?

I do not show 4 o'clock	My minute hand is pointing to the 6
I do not show half past 7	My time is half past something
My minute hand is not pointing to the 12	My hour hand is pointing between the 8 and the 9

Ask it   q

Does it show 9 o'clock?	Does it show … o'clock?
Does it show half past 8?	Does it show half past … ?
Is the minute hand pointing to the 6?	Is the hour hand pointing between … and … ?

Talk it 10

I am not a 1p coin	I am worth more than 2p
I am not a 10p coin	I am not round
I am worth more than 20p	I am worth less than £1

Ask it 10

Is it a … p coin?	Is it worth less than 50p?
Is it worth more than 2p?	Is it worth less than … p?
Is it worth more than … p?	Is it round?

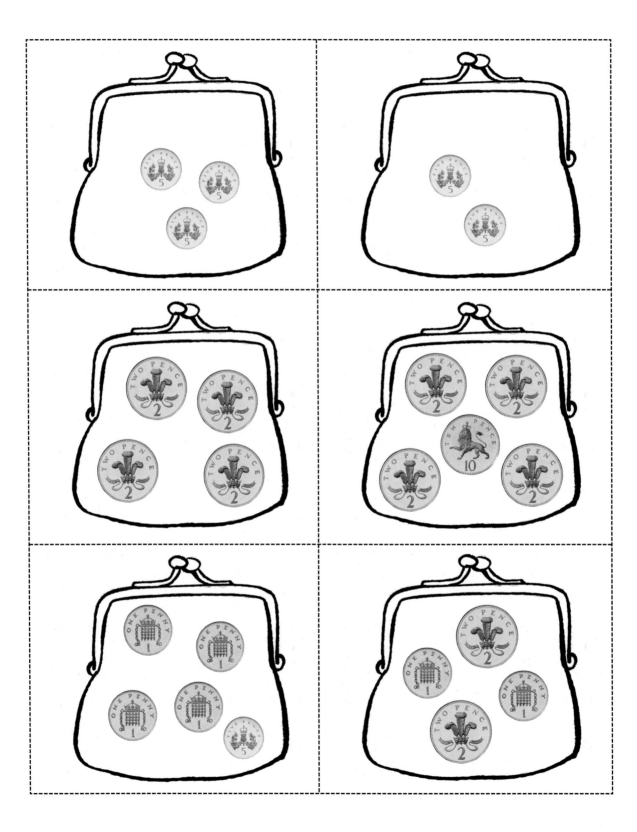

Talk it 11

I have more than two coins	My total is less than 10p
My purse is nice	I have some 1p coins
I have a 5p coin	I have five coins

Ask it 11

Has it got more than two coins?	Is the total less than ... p?
Is the total more than ... p?	Are there some 1p coins?
Are there any ... p coins?	Is the total ... p?

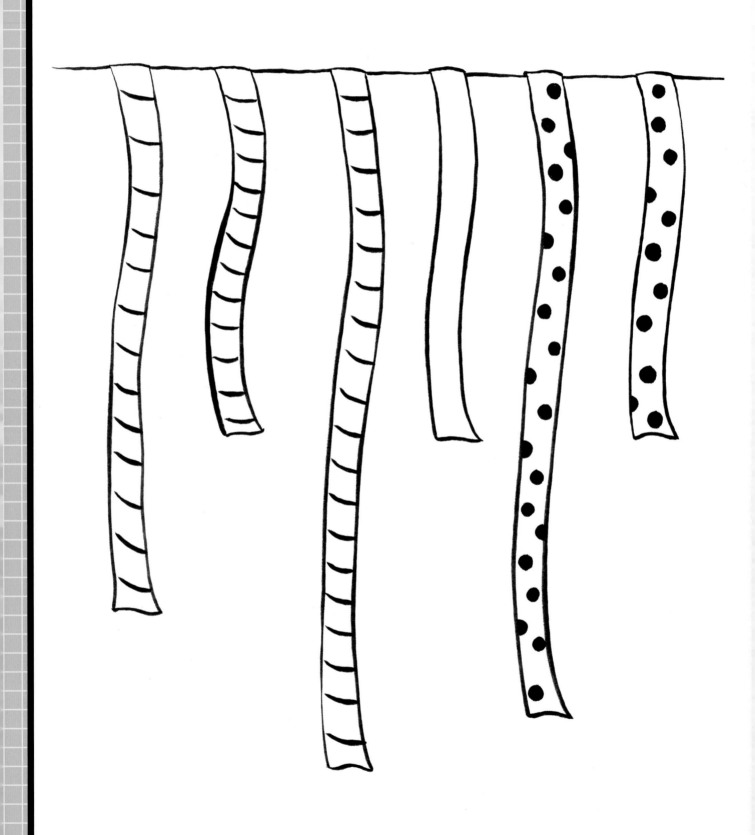

Talk it   12   Year 1

I am not the longest scarf	I am not a short scarf
I have spots	There is no other scarf the same length as me
I do not have stripes	I am not plain

Ask it   12

Is it a short scarf?	Is it the longest scarf?
Is there another scarf the same length?	Has it got spots?
Has it got stripes?	Is it plain?

Answers Year 1

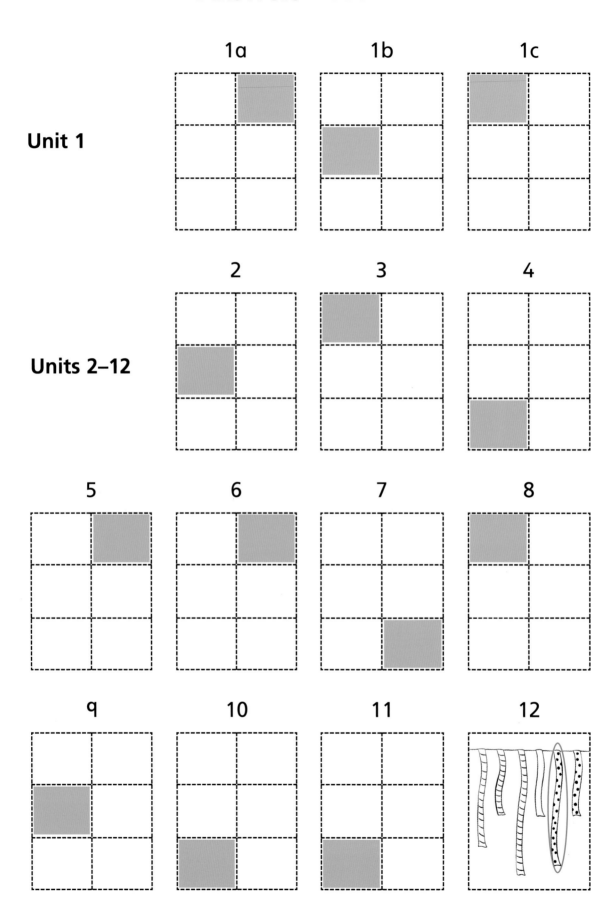

Unit 1

1a

1b

1c

Units 2–12

2

3

4

5

6

7

8

9

10

11

12

Year 2

Unit 1
Properties of 2D shapes

Unit 1 consists of the 'Solve it' sheet, three different 'Talk it' clue sheets and an 'Ask it' sheet. This unit will enable you to introduce the activity to the whole class, and to give the class confidence in using clues logically and effectively.

Talk it 1a

My flag is a rectangle	I have three portholes
Only one of my sails is a triangle	The pattern on my flag has straight lines
My portholes are hexagons	I have two sails

Talk it 1b

The pattern on my flag has curved lines	One sail has a curved side
I have ... portholes	My portholes are circles
My flag is a rectangle	One of my sails is a triangle

One sail has a curved side	My flag is a rectangle
The pattern on my flag has straight lines	I have two portholes
My portholes are square	My portholes are not hexagons

Ask it 1

Has it got three portholes?	Are its portholes square?
Are its portholes shaped like … ?	Has it got a sail shaped like a triangle?
Is its flag a … shape?	Has the pattern on its flag got … lines?

23	4
81	63
36	62

One of my digits is a 3	I'm not a one-digit number
I am an odd number	I am more than 50
I am less than 80	Add my digits and the total is 9

Ask it   2

Is it a two-digit number?	Is it an odd number?
If I add the digits, is the total … ?	Is one of the digits … ?
Is it more than … ?	Is it less than … ?

40	21
3	10
30	27

Talk it 3

I am a two-digit number	My tens digit is less than 4
I am a multiple of 10	I am more than 12
I am less than 41	I am not an odd number

Ask it 3

Is it a two-digit number?	Is it an odd number?
Is the tens digit less than ... ?	Is it a multiple of 10?
Is it more than ... ?	Is it less than ... ?

90

40

24

130

70

35

I am a two-digit number	Double me and the answer is more than 70
I am between 20 and 60	I am not odd
I am greater than 35	I am a multiple of 10

Ask it 4

Is it a two-digit number?	Is it between … and … ?
Is it even?	If I double it, is the answer less than 100?
Is it a multiple of 10?	Is it greater than … ?

12

43

25

6

35

15

Talk it 5

I am not below 20	I am a multiple of 5
I am above 21	I am greater than 20
My ones digit is 5	Add my digits and the total is 7

Ask it 5

Is it below 20?	Is it above 21?
Is it a multiple of 5?	Is it greater than … ?
Is the ones digit … ?	If I add the digits, is the total … ?

Talk it   6   Year 2

Some of my buttons are grey	More than two of my buttons are white
Less than half my buttons are black	Half my buttons are white
One quarter of my buttons are grey	Four of my buttons are white

Ask it   6

Are some of the buttons white?	Are half the buttons white?
Are one quarter of the buttons grey?	Is the number of buttons double … ?
Are one quarter of the buttons black?	Are … of the buttons … ?

The Book of Shapes

How to Draw a Rectangle

2D Shapes

Drawing Shapes

Round Things

What's My Shape?

Talk it 7

I am not a book shaped like a square	My front cover has a circle on it
I am a book shaped like a rectangle	I have a triangle on my front cover
A shape on my front cover has four right angles	I have a three-sided shape on my front cover

Ask it 7

Is the shape of the book square?	Does the front cover have a shape with four right angles?
Is there a … -sided shape on its front cover?	Does the front cover have a circle on it?
Does the front cover have a square on it?	Does the front cover have a … on it?

I am not quarter to something

Neither hand is pointing to the 12

My hour hand is pointing between the 5 and the 6

I am half past something

My minute hand is pointing to the 6

I am not quarter past something

Ask it   8

Is it quarter to something?

Is it quarter past something?

Is it half past something?

Is it 5 o'clock?

Is the minute hand pointing to ... ?

Is the hour hand pointing between ... and ... ?

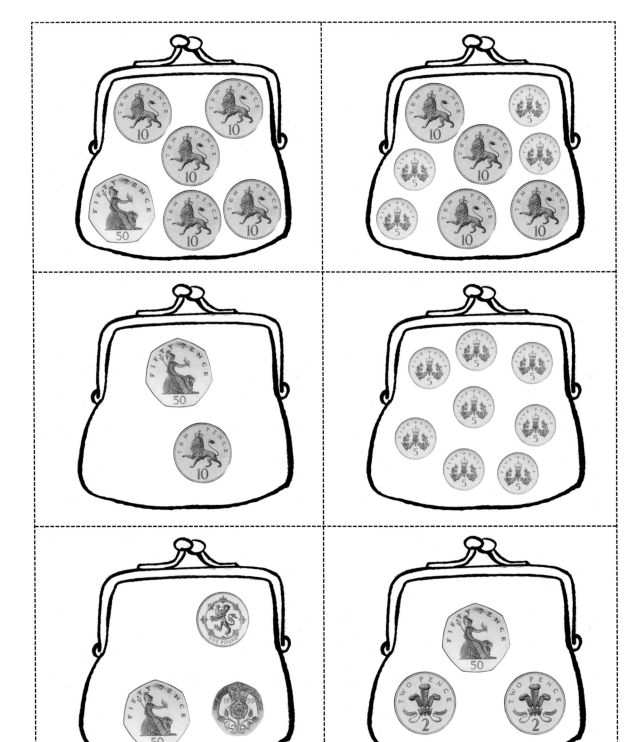

I have less than £1	One of my coins is worth five 10p coins
I have fewer than 5 coins	I have more than 50p
I have 60p	I have more than one coin

Ask it   q

Has it less than £1?	Has it more than 60p?
Is one of the coins … ?	Has it any … coins?
Has it fewer than … coins?	Has it more than … coins?

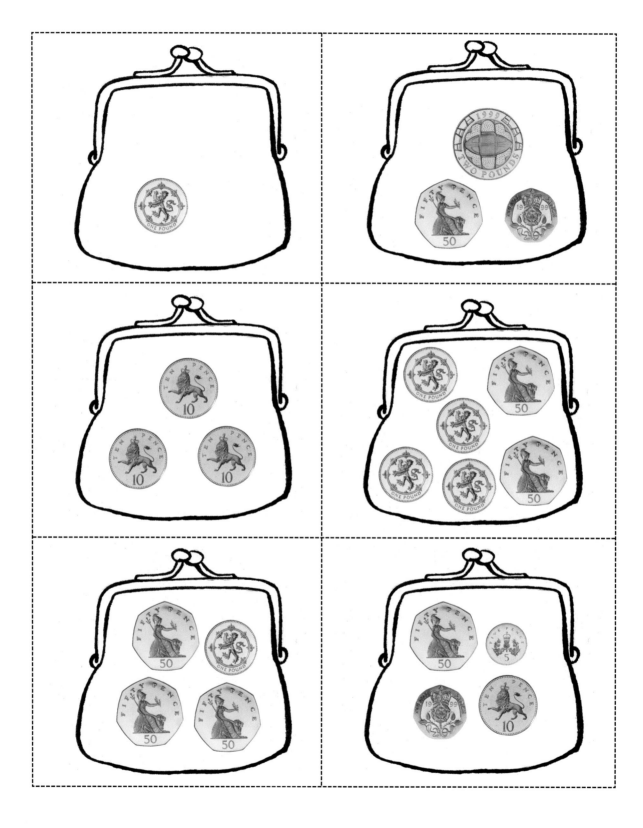

I have more than two coins	The total of my coins is more than £1
I have less than £5	One of my coins is worth ten 10p coins
I have less than £3	Three of my coins are the same

Ask it 10

Is the total of the coins more than £1?	Is the total of the coins less than £3?
Has it any ... coins?	Are ... of the coins the same?
Has it fewer than ... coins?	Has it more than ... coins?

I am not the highest bird	I am on the left side of the tree
I am next to a black bird	I am on one of the lowest branches
I am to the right of a black bird	I am a black bird

Ask it   11

Is it the highest bird?	Is it on the left side of the tree?
Is it next to a … bird?	Is it on one of the lowest branches?
Is it to the right of a … bird?	Is it a … bird?

My top is narrower than my base	I am one of the tallest mugs
My base is wider than my top	There is a pattern low on me
I am not the same width at the top and bottom	There is a pattern high on me

Ask it 12

Is its top narrower than its base?	Is its top wider than its base?
Is it one of the tallest mugs?	Is there is a pattern low on it?
Is it the same width at the top and bottom?	Is there a pattern high on it?

Answers   Year 2

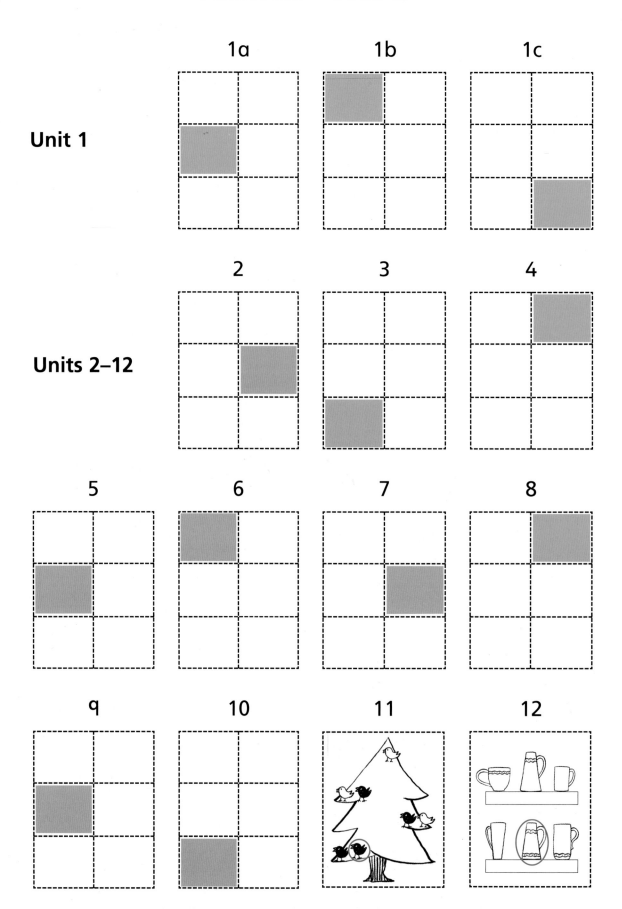

Unit 1

1a   1b   1c

Units 2–12

2   3   4

5   6   7   8

9   10   11   12